Crafts in Polyester Resin

Crafts in Polyester Resin

Herbert Scarfe

Watson-Guptill Publications   New York

First published in the United States 1973
a division of Billboard Publications Inc,
One Astor Plaza, New York, N.Y. 10036

Copyright © 1973 by Herbert Scarfe
First published 1973 in Great Britain by B T Batsford Limited,
4 Fitzhardinge Street, London W1H 0AH

Manufactured in Great Britain

Library of Congress Cataloging in Publication Data

Scarfe, Herbert
Crafts in polyester resin

Bibliography: p.
1   Plastics craft.   2   Polyesters.   I   Title.
TT297.S28 1973   745.57   72–11557
ISBN 0–8230–1004–X

First Printing 1973

Contents

Acknowledgment

Grateful thanks to my wife, Doreen, for assistance with the manuscript and resin examples; also to colleagues and friends for their advice and help in many ways.

Herbert Scarfe
Long Riston
1972

Introduction

Plastics are a familiar part of our daily lives, serving a variety of purposes. Of the many types of plastics, the special properties of polyester resins enables the material to be poured, moulded or pressed into forms which have innumerable domestic as well as industrial applications. The creative and educational uses of polyester resins are equally numerous. Here are introduced ideas and techniques for use in the school craftroom, and for the many people who are interested in the use of polyester resins as a leisure craft.

The basic techniques outlined present methods of embedding organic and inorganic objects in clear or tinted resin for study and display, progressing to further exploration of the medium as a form of creative expression. Scientific data has been kept to a minimum and the examples presented in a step-by-step form. The experimental projects are intended as suggestions to encourage individual discovery and enterprise arising out of an understanding of the nature of materials involved.

Liquid resins

The processes described in the following chapters involve the use of unsaturated polyester resins, which are thermo-setting liquids. This type of resin solidifies through a chemical change known as *polymerisation* or curing, which is a non-reversible action. Polymerisation is precipitated by an *accelerator*, sometimes called the *activator*, and a *catalyst* (hardener), and is accompanied by a rapid rise in temperature. Physical changes occur in the molecular structure of the material, progressing from liquid to gel and finally to a rigid mass. In thin sheets or layers, rigidity in the structure produces a brittle quality which may require reinforcement, and the most widely used material for this purpose is glass fibre. Degrees of viscosity can be achieved to suit the nature of the project being undertaken; for example, pouring into moulds or direct surface application.

A full range of colour, either translucent or opaque, can be produced by adding colour pigment to clear transparent resins. The hardened resin provides a versatile medium which can be machined like wood or metal, or sawn, shaped and polished as required.

SUPPLY AND STORAGE

The liquid resins are usually supplied in either metal canisters or opaque polythene containers, serving a two-fold purpose:

1 Safety in transport and storage (being inflammable material).

2 Protection of contents from exposure to light,

particularly sunlight, which shortens the active life of resins.

The *accelerator* and *catalyst* are necessary ingredients to promote curing in the resins but *they must never be mixed together or allowed to come in direct contact with each other in any way*. They are highly combustible and if combined may cause a minor explosion. It is advisable for these materials to be clearly labelled and stored separately in fireproof cupboards or boxes. When added to liquid resin in measured quantities, accelerator first followed by catalyst, they are perfectly safe. Catalyst may be obtained as a liquid or paste. Some manufacturers supply the resin in pre-activated condition, requiring only the addition of one ingredient (hardener) for curing. This greatly simplifies the mixing process and eliminates any danger of contact between accelerator and catalyst. Full instructions and adequate warnings are usually given by makers of the products. In the USA polyester resin comes pre-mixed or pre-activated, with accelerator. The amount of accelerator in the resin will *not* cause an explosion when the catalyst is added. The only danger would be from *pure* accelerator, which one would have no reason to have around when using these pre-activated resins.

The shelf life of resins can vary from six to twelve months but is considerably less for accelerator and catalyst and these should be used within six months of delivery. Storage temperatures should be about 20°C (68°F).

WORKING PRECAUTIONS

Polyester resins present few problems if used with reasonable care and the following simple precautions observed:
1 Always work in a well-ventilated room. Concentration of vapour from the resin can be unpleasant if inhaled over a prolonged period.

2   Because of the inflammable nature of the materials involved, work must not be carried out near naked flames.
3   Hands should be protected by a barrier cream to guard against the grease-solvent properties of the resins and prevent skin irritation. Acetone cleansing fluid will remove resins from the hands, followed by a wash in warm, soapy water.
4   Careful disposal of cleaning rags or papers which have been in contact with resins, catalyst or cleansing fluid is essential. Spontaneous combustion is possible if these materials are left lying around the workroom.

Encapsulation

Natural examples of encapsulation in organic resin can be seen in polished amber containing insects and fragmentary vegetation. Amber is composed of resinous deposits from coniferous trees dating far back in geological time. The liquid resin engulfed insect species and other organic materials and eventually solidified through pressure in the earth.

The process of encapsulation with polyester resins has made it possible to embed and preserve many objects from natural and man-made sources. The hardened block of resin can be highly polished to reveal the object within for study purposes or as a permanent decorative feature.

WHAT TO EMBED

Almost any object of manageable size, capable of being contained within a mould, can be successfully embedded in a cast resin block. Owing to the slightly different composition of some activated resins, certain metals such as copper may present difficulties by inhibiting the hardening process. In such instances the manufacturers will make this clear in their instruction leaflet.

Among the wide selection of objects which are frequently embedded in clear, colourless resin as trinkets or novelties are small mechanical components, coins, stamps and sea-shells. For educational purposes, minute or brittle objects such as delicate specimens of biological or mineralogical interest can be safely preserved in the hardened resin to facilitate easy handling for microscopic study.

Moulds for resin casting should have a perfectly smooth surface to avoid the need for excessive polishing later. Resin cast into smooth containers requires no polishing where the hardened block makes contact with the mould but the upper or open surface will need polishing. The exception to this will be where the open surface of a flexible mould has been covered with polythene sheet, forming contact with the resin. Such a procedure is not justified where the casting has to be removed from the mould by immersion in hot water. Shallow oven-glass dishes, thick polythene ware, polished metal containers, or any other object with a smooth interior, capable of holding liquid and withstanding high temperatures, will make suitable moulds. One of the most important things applicable to any mould is that internal projections and overhanging rims must not be present as such features make it impossible to withdraw the cast from the mould *(figure 1)*.

It is possible to obtain glazed pottery moulds specially made for resin casting which provide a selection of shapes designed for easy release of the castings. Polystyrene and some types of plastic containers of a thin, brittle nature are unsuitable for use as moulds.

Specimens can be successfully set within rounded or dome-shaped moulds and the curved dome of the casting will assist in magnification for detailed study. For objects where any distortion is undesirable, flat moulds should be used.

MIXING THE RESINS

Precise proportions of liquid resin, accelerator and catalyst cannot be stated in general terms as most manu-facturers have an individual formula for their product, with special instructions for mixing.

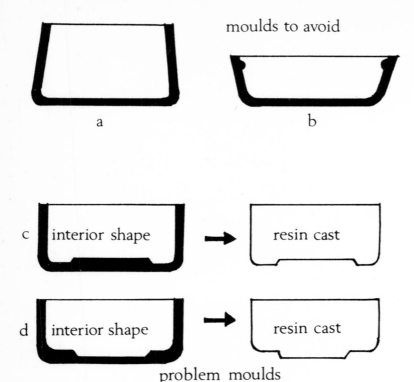

moulds to avoid

problem moulds

good mould shape

FIGURE 1 Mould shapes.
(a) Sides tapering inwards. *(b)* Small flange or rim inside dish. Removal of casting impossible without breaking mould. *(c) and (d)* Castings will require laborious shaping and sanding to level off. *(e)* Good features: wider at opening with smooth, even sides and rounded corners for easy waxing and release

However, in every case, allowances are made for experimentation with the quantity of catalyst, which can be increased or decreased slightly. For example, when embedding a delicate specimen which might be affected by the rise in temperature during curing the amount of catalyst should be kept to a minimum. If too little is added, or if not sufficiently well-mixed, the curing time will be prolonged or may even lead to permanently soft, sticky areas. On the other hand, too much catalyst will increase the thermal action, causing rapid curing which may produce cracking in the casting.

WHAT HAPPENS WITHIN THE MOULD

A coating of releasing wax spread over the interior surface of the mould acts as a barrier between mould and resin. Without wax the resin would adhere to a rigid mould, making removal of the casting difficult if not impossible, short of breaking the mould. Releasing wax is not required for polythene moulds as antipathy between smooth polythene and resin reduces the problems of release.

The liquid resin will conform exactly to the interior shape of a mould and the hardened casting will echo the surface texture. A perfectly smooth mould will produce a polished casting. On the other hand, any change of shape such as a minute rim or embossed trade mark will be repeated. Even raised wax smears not removed by polishing the mould will be reproduced on the casting.

Most encapsulation techniques require two or more stages, filling the mould with separate layers of resin, each of which is allowed to harden thoroughly. Thick layers or castings above 25mm (1 in.) should not be attempted at one application as heat generated within the block may lead to splitting or crazing. The risk can be minimised by reducing the quantity of hardener or by curing slowly in a cool temperature. Recent advances in polyester resin technology have made it possible to obtain resins suitable for casting larger masses at one application and for big projects the use of this type of resin is advisable.

The resin poured into a mould as a first layer will find its own level and it is important to ensure that this is horizontal by placing the mould on a flat surface, particularly when using a coloured base layer. If insufficient resin has been mixed to achieve the desired level in the mould, allow to set completely. Do not attempt to add a little more from a second mixing while the first mix is still liquid. It will already have started to cure and will continue at a different rate to the second mix.

As polymerisation takes place, with a considerable rise in temperature, the liquid resin gradually gels and assumes a globular composition with uneven rippled surface. If the mould is tilted at this stage the whole jelly mass will move. When curing is completed the resin will have set into a rigid block but the exposed surface of the layer will remain tacky and must not be disturbed unduly when arranging the object for embedding. This tackiness assists bonding of the next layer of resin and eliminates any evidence of a division. Shrinkage of between ten to twenty per cent of the resin may occur during hardening. This will be in evidence on surfaces exposed to air but does not usually take place where the casting is in contact with a rigid mould.

Always pour the resin slowly to prevent formation of bubbles. These invariably disappear during setting but some may lodge on the specimen and remain as trapped air pockets. Bubbles can be dispersed while the resin is still liquid by tapping the mould or probing. When a flat object is placed on the first hardened layer, air bubbles trapped under the specimen during application of the second layer of resin must be removed. This can be done by moving the object about in the liquid and lifting the edge with tweezers to release the air.

16

Make sure the room in which work is to be carried out is well ventilated. Allow a clear working space for preparation of specimens and resin. Cover table surface with newspapers and have an orderly arrangement of materials. Work methodically and remember to add activator and/or hardener according to the maker's instructions. Ensure that all containers are airtight when not in use and keep cleansing fluids, resins and additives away from naked flames.

MATERIALS REQUIRED

Suitable mould. Heat resistant and large enough to contain specimen
Mould release wax to coat interior of rigid moulds
Liquid resin. Clear casting type, preferably pre-activated
Accelerator (for use only if resin is not pre-activated type)
Catalyst (hardener) to add to activated resin
Colour pigments (readily obtainable as pastes) supplied in translucent and opaque colour range
Preserving fluids for organic specimens
Tweezers for handling delicate objects
Stirring sticks or spatulas
Disposable mixing cups e.g. foil containers or waxed cartons
Measuring beaker of glass or polythene to measure exact quantities of resin and additives
Cleansing fluid such as acetone, to remove resin from hands and containers
Cleaning materials. Tissues, paper towels, liquid detergent

Embedding inorganic objects

Hard, non-absorbent objects such as metallic forms, pebbles, coins and crystal specimens present few problems during the embedding process providing they are clean, dry and free from grease. If the object is very cold, cracking of the resin can occur. The curing process starts immediately and variation in temperature between object and resin may set up a series of tensions but this can be avoided by warming the object slightly prior to embedding.

Castings are often formed in reverse order, the object being set in an inverted position and the open or upper end of the mould forms the base of the hardened resin block. The following example shows how to overcome the problem of inverting an irregular object, such as a crystal specimen, for setting within a domed mould (*figure 2*).

FIGURE 2   Inorganic specimen

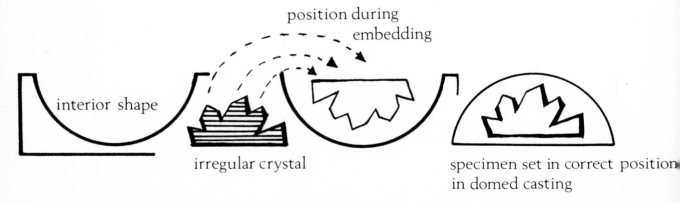

position during embedding

interior shape

irregular crystal

specimen set in correct position in domed casting

Stage one (figure 3)

1   Coat mould with wax and polish with soft cloth.

2   Measure out sufficient resin to fill bottom of mould, using plastic measure or glass beaker. Add activator and/or hardener (catalyst).

   (a)   If resin is not pre-activated, correct amount of activator must be added and stirred before addition of hardener.

   (b)   Add hardener and stir well into resin.

3   Pour resin into mould to form a shallow layer.

4   Cover mould to prevent dust forming on surface of resin. Ensure level of liquid is horizontal. Leave until hard.

FIGURE 3   Stage one

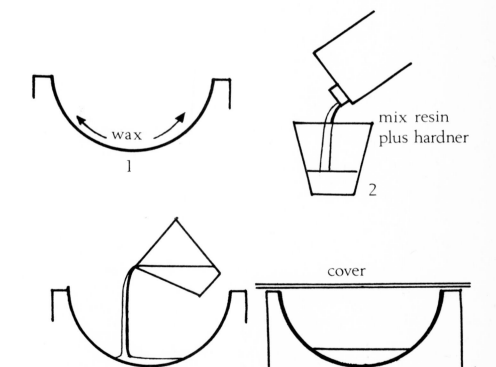

wax

1

mix resin
plus hardner

2

3

cover

4

Stage two (figure 4)

5   Suspend object by thread from a short stick placed across mould. Allow object to touch hardened resin layer and secure in position.

6   Mix resin as before and pour second layer into mould. Just immerse tip of object, which will be firmly anchored in position as setting occurs. Remove any air bubbles. Cover and allow to set.

7   When resin is completely set the thread can be removed. Object will now be fixed in position.

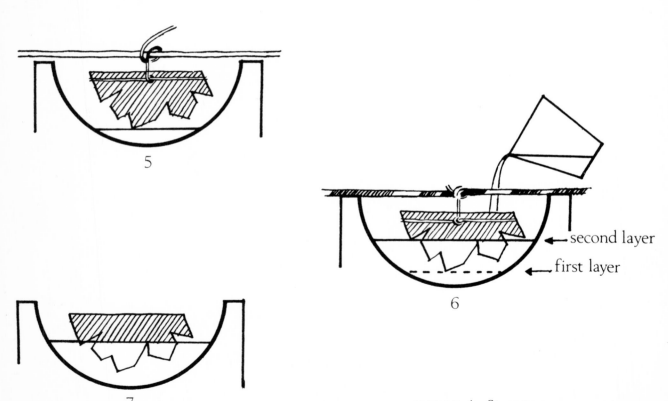

FIGURE 4   Stage two

FIGURE 5   Stage three

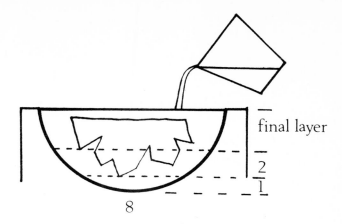

Stage three (figure 5)
8   Mix and pour in final layer of resin until level with top of mould, or to cover specimen. When thoroughly hard the division of the three layers will not be visible.

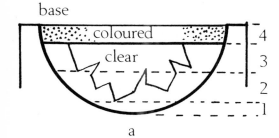

a

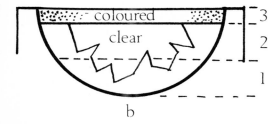

b

FIGURE 6   Coloured layer

Coloured layer (figure 6)
If a coloured base layer is required, pigment can be added to the clear resin mix for application as a fourth layer when the third has set. This can be opaque or translucent.

If the mould is shallow and a coloured layer is required, the clear resin can be applied in two stages only. This can be achieved by suspending the object and fixing it in position with the first layer of resin. For mixing, see chapter on coloured resins (page 39).

To release the casting from a rigid mould immerse in boiling or very hot water for five to ten minutes. Transfer the mould into cold water for a similar period. The resin cast will now have been released from direct contact with the mould and can easily be removed.

The base of the casting will be cloudy from contact with water and slightly concave due to shrinkage, and will need to be levelled off and polished.

FIGURE 7 Selection of tumble-polished stones too small for jewelry but attractive when set collectively in clear resin

FIGURE 8   Embedded mineral
specimens.   *Above left* Garnet
crystals.   *Above right* Marcasite
nodule. Crystal forms can be clearly
observed through the resin.
Below left Iron pyrites and marcasite.
Below right Sample of ruby in a
matrix of green zoisite

Embedding organic specimens

Organic matter must be preserved and thoroughly dried before embedding in resin. Failure to make adequate preparation may cause cloudiness to form around the specimen and gradual shrinkage which continues after the resin has cured. Distortion will occur and the space between hardened resin and specimen produces a silvery layer which obscures the form. In order to prevent such disappointments and obviate the risk of spoiling a good specimen, a trial is recommended with something less valuable.

Following dehydration, specimens are extremely brittle and delicacy in handling is essential. Colour changes and even loss of colour may be expected in some materials when immersed in preserving fluids or during contact with activated resins.

FIGURE 9 Sea-horse embedded for all-round study, revealing perfection of form

Insects, starfish, crabs and similar forms can be preserved in spirit solutions such as alcohol and formalin. The specimen may need to be arranged and fixed in a particular position before the dehydration process. This can be done by carefully placing the specimen on a mounting board and securing the legs or other movable parts in the desired position with pins. The pins should not pierce the specimen and can be inserted at angles or crossed if necessary to prevent movement or flotation. When secured, the mounted specimen is placed in a fixing solution of fifty to seventy per cent alcohol or ten to twenty per cent formalin and water until it becomes rigid. After the fixing period, remove pins and rinse the specimen in clean water.

FIGURE 10   Crab and shell forms seen through clear resin against a translucent green resin background

DEHYDRATION

FIGURE 11   Everlasting flowers

The specimen is subjected to a series of alcohol solutions, commencing with immersion in fifty per cent alcohol and water, followed by seventy per cent, ninety per cent and finally pure alcohol. A period of ten to twelve hours can be allowed for each phase. The moisture within the specimen is gradually replaced by alcohol which evaporates during the drying process at a moderately warm temperature. Once dehydration is completed the specimen must be stored in a moisture-free atmosphere until required for embedding. Some manufacturers recommend further impregnation using liquid resin without activator or hardener. When required for use, surplus resin is allowed to drain away from the specimen by placing it on an absorbent surface. At this stage the specimen can be placed directly on a previously hardened resin layer and the embedding phases continued with resin plus hardener.

PRESERVING FLOWERS

Solutions for preserving colours in freshly cut flowers, prior to embedding, can be obtained from resin suppliers in a numbered or coded range. Separate solutions are used for preserving flowers in particular colour groupings. The flower specimens should be carefully suspended in the solution for the length of time recommended in the maker's instructions, and thoroughly dried upon removal. Embedding can begin immediately or the specimen can be stored for a short period in a warm, dry atmosphere. As the preserved flowers will be extremely brittle, extra care must be used in handling and storage.

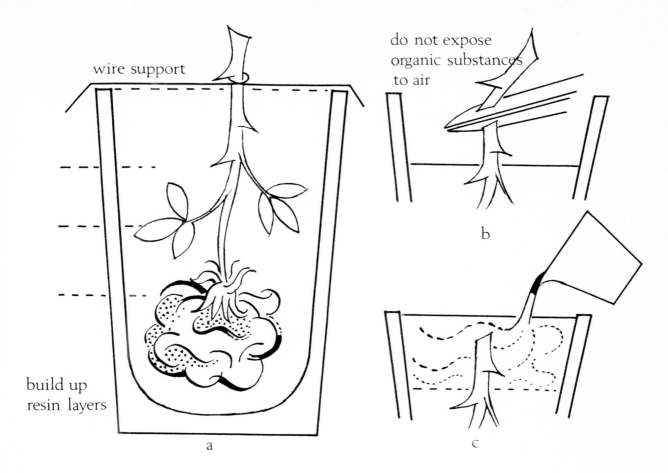

wire support

do not expose
organic substances
to air

build up
resin layers

a

b

c

FIGURE 12   Method of supporting
long-stemmed flower during
immersion in preserving fluid, also
for encapsulation in resin.
(a) Stem supported by wire.
(b) Snip off end of stem before
adding final layer.
(c) Pour in final resin layer to seal
stem completely. This layer will be
the base of the casting and may be
coloured

As an alternative method of preservation, flowers can
be covered with silica gel in a container which is then
tightly sealed. The specimens should be left undisturbed
until they are completely dry.

Display boxes containing preserved insects, such as beetles, moths and butterflies, are sometimes damaged or specimens spoiled through mishandling. Although the value of the collection as a whole may be diminished some of the specimens may still be worth preserving by permanently embedding in resin. By so doing, the opportunities for examination are greatly increased as the hardened block of resin can be handled without fear of damage to the specimen and observation of the underside as well as the upper surface is now possible.

When embedding organic specimens of this kind it is important to remember that they are thoroughly dry and brittle and will not withstand manipulation of legs, wings or other features which have not previously been arranged symmetrically. Since the density of the insects will be less than the resin, the second resin layer must be extremely shallow to prevent the specimen floating to the surface.

Procedure

The example selected is a beetle, previously dried and mounted in a display case *(figure 13)*.

FIGURE 13   Organic specimen

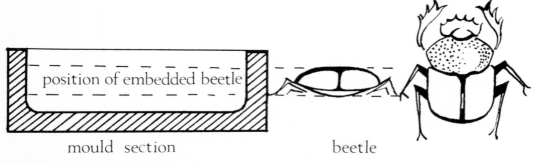

mould section   beetle

Stage one (figure 14)

1 Wax interior of mould, taking care to include corners. Polish with a soft cloth.

2 Mix liquid resin according to maker's instructions. Pour into mould to pre-determined height.

Cover to make dustproof and place on level surface to harden.

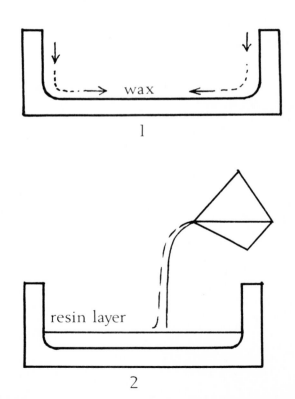

FIGURE 14 Stage one

Stage two (figure 15)

3   Anchorage layer. Mix enough resin to cover first layer with only a thin film of liquid.

4   *(a)*   Arrange specimen. Lift insect with tweezers, place carefully in liquid film. Slide into correct position.
(b)   Too much liquid will allow specimen to float on surface. Keep under observation until resin reaches a gel state to ensure that specimen remains in place. Cover until set.

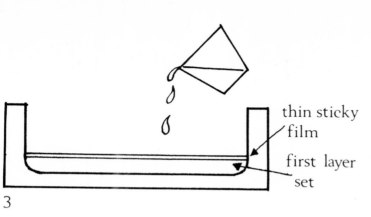

thin sticky
film

first layer
set

3

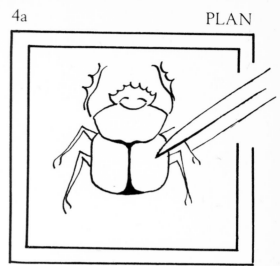

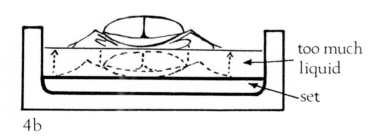

too much
liquid

set

4b

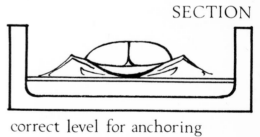

SECTION

correct level for anchoring

FIGURE 15 Stage two

Stage three (figure 16)

5   Mix resin for another layer to cover specimen partially. Tap mould gently to release any pockets of trapped air. Allow to set.

6   Mix resin for final layer to cover specimen to a reasonable depth. Allow to harden thoroughly.

Release casting from mould, using hot and cold water treatment previously described. Level off and polish top of the resin block.

PLATE 1   Examples of encapsulation of natural objects ▶

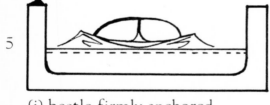

(i) beetle firmly anchored

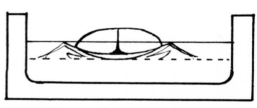

(ii) additional resin layer

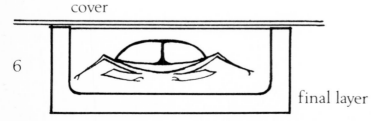

FIGURE 16   Stage three

FIGURE 17 Group of dried seed
heads embedded in clear resin

Polishing technique

After curing, any part of the resin block which was not in contact with the smooth mould may have a rippled surface and be slightly concave due to shrinkage. Immersion in water during the releasing process will also have clouded the exposed surface. By using the following methods of sanding and polishing by hand, these irregularities can soon be overcome.

SANDING

Before a final polish can be achieved, scratches and all surface imperfections have to be eliminated. This is done by using coated abrasives such as silicon carbide wet/dry papers, commencing with 220 grade and followed by finer grades of 400 and 600. (Grades are referred to as grits in the USA.) The numbers refer to the grading of abrasive grit particles; as the numbers increase the grits become finer so that each successive stage will remove marks from the previous stage until the surface appears scratch free to the naked eye. Although the hardened resin is tough it is soft in terms of resistance to abrasion and scratches easily. For this reason it is not advisable to commence abrasion with coarse sandpaper used for sanding wood as the resultant scratches would be difficult to remove. Finer grades of silicon carbide wet/dry papers will produce an even finish, and as water is used in the sanding process there are no dust problems.

Sanding procedure

Select the coarser grade (220) wet/dry paper and sprinkle a little water on the surface. Holding the resin block firmly, rub the face of the casting on the abrasive sheet. Using medium pressure, alternate between circular and figure-of-eight movements. Rinse frequently with clean water to clear the accumulation of creamy deposits from the sanded block and examine progress. When the surface is perfectly level, scratches left by the 220 abrasive will have to be removed. Change to a 400 grade paper and proceed as before, gradually refining the surface texture of the resin. Complete the sanding stage on a finer paper (600 grade), using less pressure, until a silky smooth finish is obtained. At this stage the resin will still have a dull appearance.

POLISHING

Providing the surface of the resin block is perfectly smooth and all visible scratches have been removed in the finer sanding stage, polishing it will be a simple matter. Prepare a smooth pad of cotton material stretched over a firm support. Apply a small quantity of liquid metal polish, evenly distributed over the pad, and start to polish the resin face. Rub vigorously, re-charging the pad with metal polish when this has worked into the material. Continue until the resin has acquired a good shine. A high gloss can now be obtained by rubbing the resin surface on a piece of dry velvet or other soft material.

While this is not an essential piece of equipment, it will be found that securing the sanding papers in a simple wooden frame facilitates handling and lessens the possibility of wrinkling or tearing the sheets during use. A rectangular frame can easily be constructed with mitred corners and rebated section resembling the back of a picture frame. In fact, a small picture frame could be utilised for this purpose. A piece of hardboard, fibreboard, composite board, or plywood is cut to fit into the recess *(figure 18)*. The dimensions of the frame should be slightly less than a sheet of wet/dry paper, allowing for a small wrapover on the hardboard or plywood support. This will secure the abrasive sheets in the frame and provide a rigid base for sanding. Small rubber stops or strips can be fastened to the underside of the frame to prevent slipping.

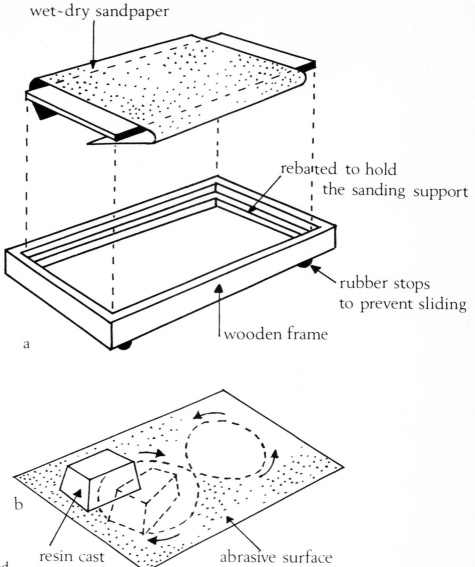

wet-dry sandpaper

rebated to hold
the sanding support

rubber stops
to prevent sliding

wooden frame

a

resin cast

abrasive surface

b

FIGURE 18 *(a)* Sanding and polishing frame. *(b)* Sanding movement for a flat surface

FIGURE 19 Coloured resin, showing attractive variations possible when shaped and polished

Coloured resin

A full range of colour in both opaque and translucent form, together with metallic pastes and powders, can be obtained for tinting the clear liquid resins. These are specially prepared for use with polyester resins, having stability and fastness to light.

MIXING

The colour pigment is usually supplied with a consistency of thick cream or paste and can be added to quantities of liquid resin with a small spatula or stirring stick. Mixing cups such as aluminium foil containers, which are ideal for this purpose, should be available for each colour to be mixed, as well as separate mixing sticks.

Measure out a quantity of liquid resin into a suitable container and introduce the required percentage of hardener. The process of polymerisation will now have commenced and the mixing period is limited before the resin begins to gel. For this reason, do not attempt to accomplish more than is possible within the time. Pour some of the clear resin into a mixing cup and with a clean, dry stick add a little of the selected colour pigment and stir well. If additional pigment is required to intensify the colour mixture, clean the activated resin from the spatula to avoid transferring it to the colour paste. The colour mixture can be poured directly into a mould to form a base layer, or used for tinting larger quantities of resin.

INTENSE COLOUR   INTENSE COLOUR

mix first   PRIMARY COLOURS

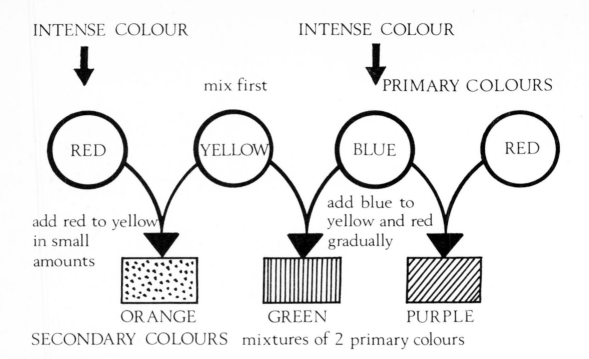

RED   YELLOW   BLUE   RED

add red to yellow in small amounts

add blue to yellow and red gradually

ORANGE   GREEN   PURPLE

SECONDARY COLOURS   mixtures of 2 primary colours

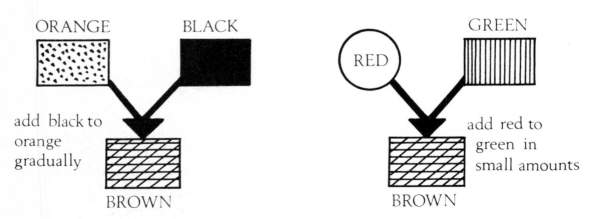

ORANGE   BLACK   GREEN

add black to orange gradually

RED

add red to green in small amounts

BROWN   BROWN

FIGURE 20 (*opposite*) Mixing colours. Colour pastes are produced in brilliant colours. The intensity of primary and secondary colours can be subdued by mixing to obtain a more subtle colour range

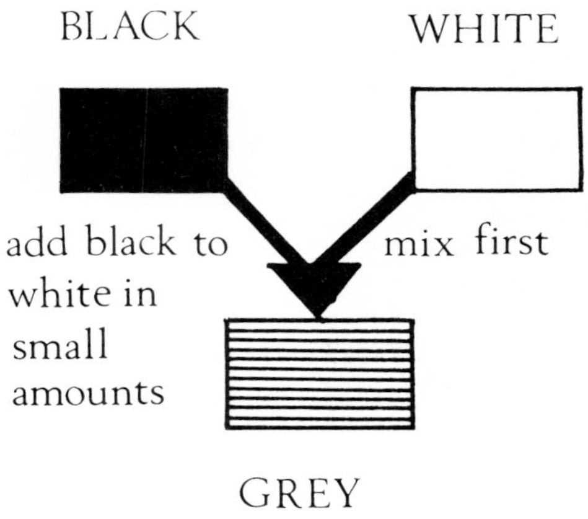

BLACK   WHITE

add black to
white in
small
amounts   mix first

GREY

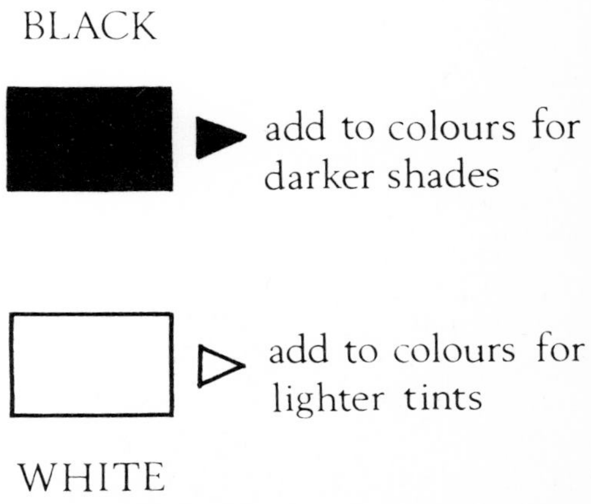

BLACK

add to colours for
darker shades

FIGURE 21   Tonal variation. Intermix small amounts of secondary colours or secondary and primary colours to vary the tonal range and produce colour tints and shades. To reduce colour intensity, a small amount of grey added to the colours will act as a neutraliser and give a more harmonious range

add to colours for
lighter tints

WHITE

41

The opaque colours are miscible should more subtle variations be required, and by adding white or black in small amounts a wide range of colour tints and shades can be obtained. In the translucent colour range intermixing of colours is less effective owing to the reduced colour pigmentation. A translucent effect can be achieved by lightly tinting clear resin with opaque colour. When mixing colours together, use a different spatula for each one and ensure that the sticks are clean and dry to prevent contamination of the colour pastes.

Although it is possible to mix the colour and liquid resin before introducing the hardener, it is recommended that each colour should be mixed with small amounts of activated resin *plus* hardener. This will ensure that the volume of colour does not upset the balanced ratio of resin to hardener when the colour mix is added to the bulk of clear resin. Failure to do this may result in soft colour patches within the hardened resin which remain permanently tacky. Further sticky colour patches can arise from inadequate mixing of pigment and resin. Sanding and polishing are impossible under these conditions.

USES FOR COLOURED RESIN

A uniformly-coloured resin may be required for the base or supporting layer during encapsulation. The colour pigment should be stirred well into the activated resin until all traces of colour separation and streaks have disappeared before pouring into the mould. For swirled or marbled effects, allow a resin layer to gel partially and introduce globules of different colours. Using a pointed stick, swirl the colours in the near-gelled mass until a suitable pattern has been formed *(see colour plate 2)*. Colours dribbled on the surface of clear or tinted resin which has not quite reached a gel stage, will be activated into randon patterns without the need for stirring. Colour may also be forced into a near gelled mass of resin by injection, giving a controlled directional pattern. Syringes used for this must be cleaned thoroughly immediately after use with a solvent such as acetone, followed by a hot water and detergent rinse.

The success of experimental pattern formation with coloured resins will depend on the condition of the resin and the stage of curing when the colour is introduced. The best results are obtained when the resin has reached a near gel state, permitting colour suspension. If the resin is too liquid when the colour is added, the concentration of pigment will sink to the base of the mould.

Creative encapsulation

Used imaginatively, the techniques previously described for embedding can be further extended as a creative process. Original designs can be made from the simplest forms; for example, nut shells, dried grasses, poppy heads and hollow-stemmed plants. By filling natural cavities or hollow stem sections with coloured resins, decorative elements can be produced for encapsulation. The ideas which follow have been developed to show some of the possibilities of the medium used in this way. Experimentation on similar lines will produce many other projects which can be utilised for a variety of ornamental purposes.

MATERIALS REQUIRED

A sharp craft knife
Small hacksaw
Flexible polythene bottles (type used for liquid detergents)
Roll of cellulose tape (*Sellotape* or *Scotchtape*)
Piece of thick card to use as cutting board
Usual materials for preparation of coloured resins
Empty peanut shells
Dried hemlock stems (plastic drinking straws, hollow marsh weeds or lengths of bamboo make good substitutes)

EXAMPLE 1   HEMLOCK STEM SECTIONS

Following their season of fruitfulness, hemlock plants can be seen in fields and hedgerows in Britain as dried skeletal forms, their rigid hollow stems standing like fluted columns. The main stems and diminishing branches will provide a selection of hollow tubes of varying diameters which can be cut into short lengths *(figure 22)*. Trimming and cutting of the plants should be done outdoors to shake free any insects concealed in the hollow stems.

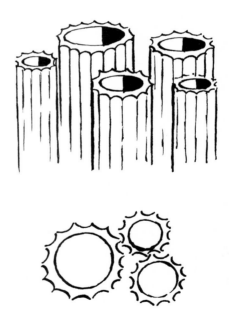

FIGURE 22   Hemlock stems showing hollow tubes. Cross-section pattern of fluted sides

Cut off the lower portion of a polythene bottle and insert short lengths of hemlock stems until the space within the container is tightly packed (*figure 23*). Mix small amounts of coloured resins and carefully fill up the hollow tubes of hemlock. Drops of different colours can be added to produce random colour mixtures if desired. When the hollow stems are filled, direct the coloured resins into the spaces in between to fill the polythene container completely.To control the resin during pouring, allow the liquid to run down a thin piece of stick held at an angle with one end inserted into the cavity to be filled.

When the resin has thoroughly set, cut away the polythene to expose a rigid cylindrical block (*figure 24*).

FIGURE 23   Tightly packed stems in polythene container

FIGURE 24   Removing the polythene from the resin block

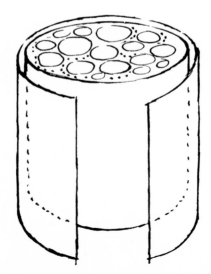

FIGURE 25 Slicing and trimming
the hardened resin into desired shapes

Hold the resin block securely and saw a number of parallel slices with a small hacksaw. If colour mixing has been introduced no two sections will be alike, giving contrast to the fluted and circular patterns of the stems. By varying the angle of cut the shapes of the patterned sections will range from circles to elongated ovals *(figures 25 and 26)*.

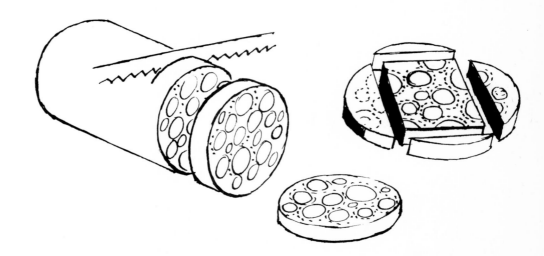

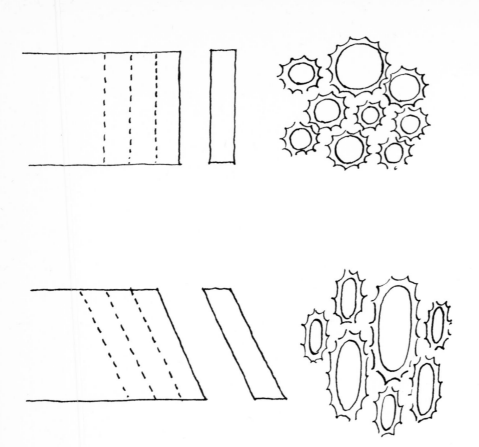

FIGURE 26   Varying the angle of the cut to produce elongated ovals

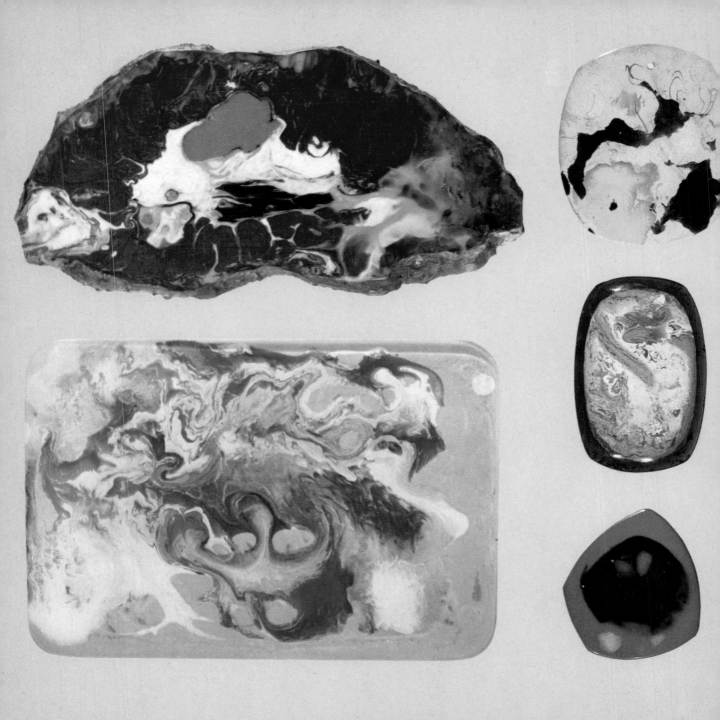

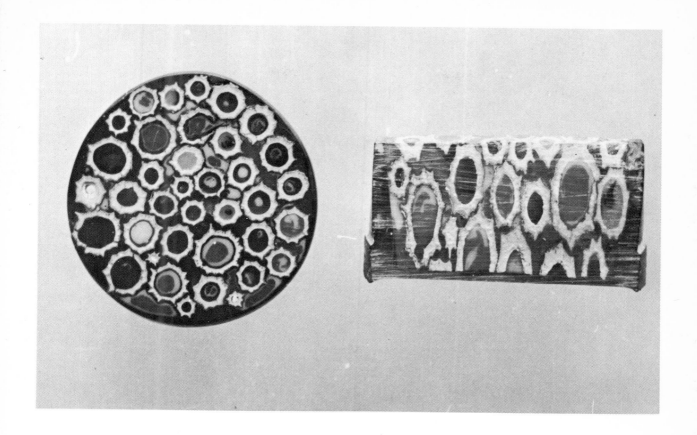

PLATE 2 Coloured resin. *Left* The resin cast in slabs. *Right* Pieces shaped and polished for jewelry

FIGURE 27 The treated hemlock stems shaped and polished

To complete the project the trimmed sections are totally encapsulated in clear resin, or can be arranged on a coloured resin background and covered with transparent resin. The sections of hemlock must be completely immersed in resin to prevent decomposition of the organic material. When the resin has hardened it can be shaped and polished as required.

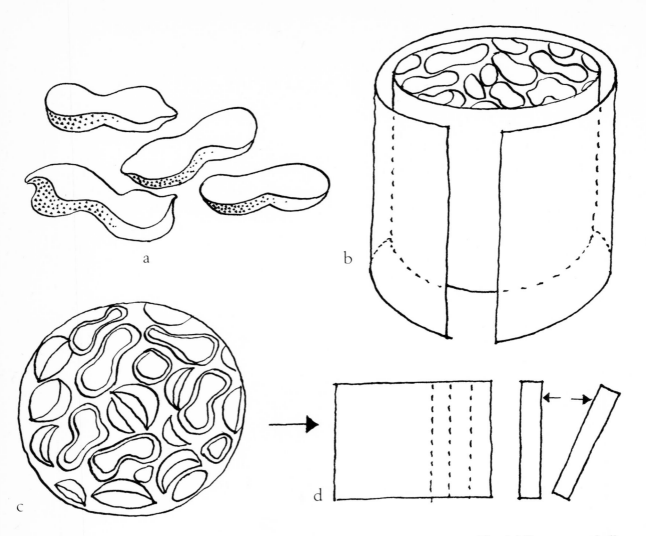

FIGURE 28 (a) Empty nut shells as receptacles for coloured resins. (b) Tightly packed shells embedded in resin block. Polythene container cut and peeled away. (c) Cross-section of slice cut from block (d)

EXAMPLE 2 PEANUT SHELL SECTIONS

The procedure used here is similar to that used in the previous example; the main difference being that the hollow peanut shells are filled with coloured resins and allowed to set prior to packing into the polythene bottle container. When closely packed, the spaces around the peanut shells are filled with coloured resin and allowed to set as before *(figure 28)*.

Upon removal from the container the resin block is sawn into sections as required. As a further variation for embedding, half sections of two corresponding faces will give symmetrically balanced patterns which can be used in any number of different designs. The shapes are then encapsulated in clear resin *(figures 29 and 30)*.

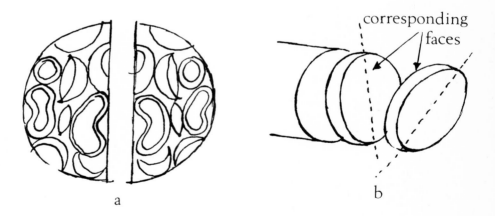

a

corresponding faces

b

FIGURE 29   *(a)* Pattern symmetry of two corresponding half-sections, from the same saw-cut *(b)*

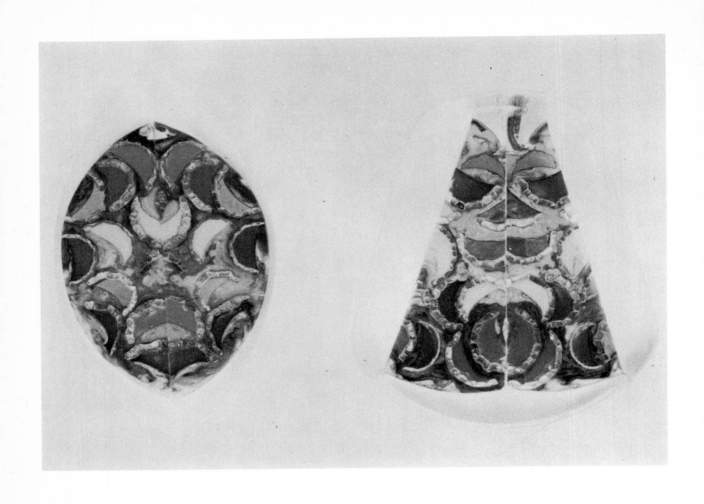

FIGURE 30 Corresponding half-sections encapsulated in clear resin

EXAMPLE 3 POLYTHENE BOTTLE SECTIONS

Cut away the central portion from a flexible polythene
bottle; the length will depend upon the number of
sections desired. Depress the polythene and push the
resultant curve until it meets the opposite face of the
container. Fold the flexible material round to form the
shape illustrated in figure 31. Secure the shape with strips
of cellulose adhesive. The open base must then be sealed
with a piece of polythene and strips of adhesive tape to
prevent leakage of resin. Support the container in an
upright position and fill the cavity shapes with coloured
resins.

FIGURE 31 Folding the flexible
material and securing with tape

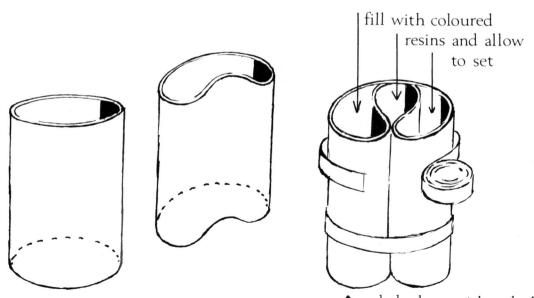

fill with coloured
resins and allow
to set

↑ seal the base with polythene
and cellulose tape to prevent leakage

53

When the resin is set, do not remove the polythene at this stage but saw into slices with a hacksaw (*figure 32*). The resin shapes can then be pushed out of the polythene strips and arranged into patterns.

FIGURE 32 *(a)* Slicing with a hacksaw and *(b)* arranging for embedding

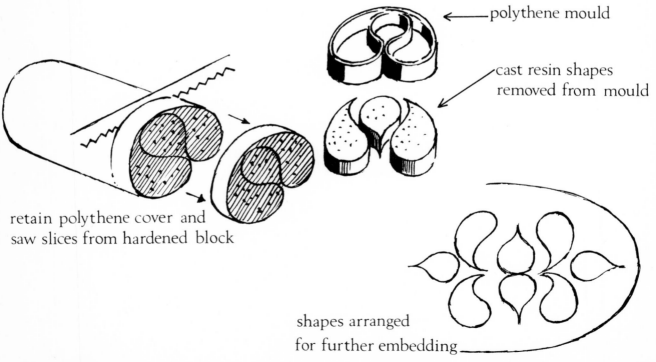

polythene mould

cast resin shapes removed from mould

retain polythene cover and saw slices from hardened block

shapes arranged for further embedding

Form a retaining wall of any suitable shape with strips cut from polythene bottles and secure to a base of polythene or waxed glass, sealing any junctions with plasticine or cellulose tape. Pour in a thin layer of coloured resin and allow to gel or reach a tacky stage. Place the resin shapes on the tacky surface in the pre-determined pattern and leave until stuck into position. Fill the spaces between the shapes with resin until the surface is level. Cover and allow to set thoroughly. Remove the resin block from the polythene strip mould and sand and polish the entire surface. An attractive decorative plaque, paperweight or a pendant can be produced in this way, depending on the thickness and size (*figure 33*).

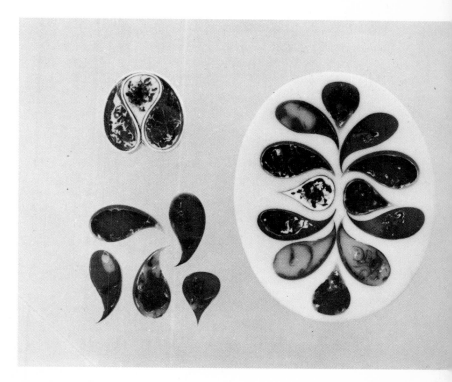

FIGURE 33 *Top left* Slice through a resin block cast in a polythene bottle. *Below* Some of the shapes isolated for trial arrangements. *Right* Shapes arranged into a design and embedded in a white resin background

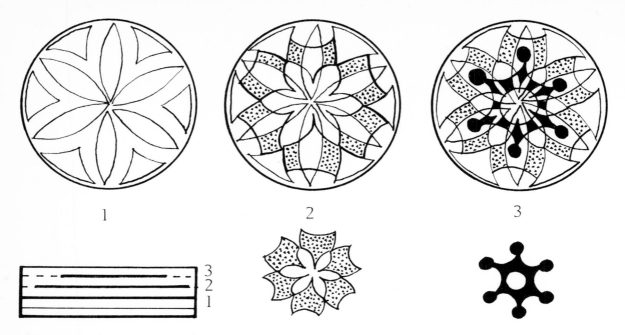

1   2   3

shapes embedded at 3 levels

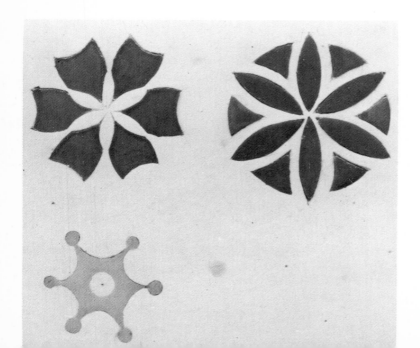

FIGURE 34 Planned symmetry.
A design project developed by
superimposing three motifs
embedded at different levels in clear
resin. Motifs are cast in transparent
coloured resin of contrasting tone
(see *figure 35*). Light reflected from
a white base layer is transmitted
upwards through the coloured shapes

FIGURE 35 Transparent coloured
motifs cast in shallow moulds
carved in a tray of plaster of paris.
Different colour combinations can
be cast from the same moulds

Resin jewelry

In jewelry, coloured resins can be used to perform many of the decorative functions of gemstones and enamels, or combine with these and other materials. Blocks of resin can be sawn, shaped and polished in the manner of gemstones and techniques are often identical. In liquid form, resins can be poured into cavities or contained within a pattern of shallow moulds in much the same way as *cloissoné* enamelling. In addition to the methods described using polyester resins of the clear casting and moulding type, it is possible to obtain a cold setting liquid plastic which simulates many of the characteristics of vitreous enamels, such as resistance to abrasion, high colour gloss and fastness to light. All the traditional enamelling techniques are possible with this cold setting material, dispensing with the usual kiln and firing problems.

Making jewelry with the simplest of equipment, in some cases involving no more than pouring resin into moulds cut from discarded polythene containers, has a wide appeal for children. As familiarity with the medium increases, greater flexibility and control will follow and creation of resin jewelry will provide a satisfactory outlet for imagination and technical ingenuity. Groups of children, under supervision in the preparation of the resins, can participate in designing and fashioning items for personal adornment or as costume jewelry for drama productions.

Methods of mounting the 'jewels' are numerous and resin can easily be drilled for a variety of fastenings or hangings. Alternatively, chains or leather thongs can be

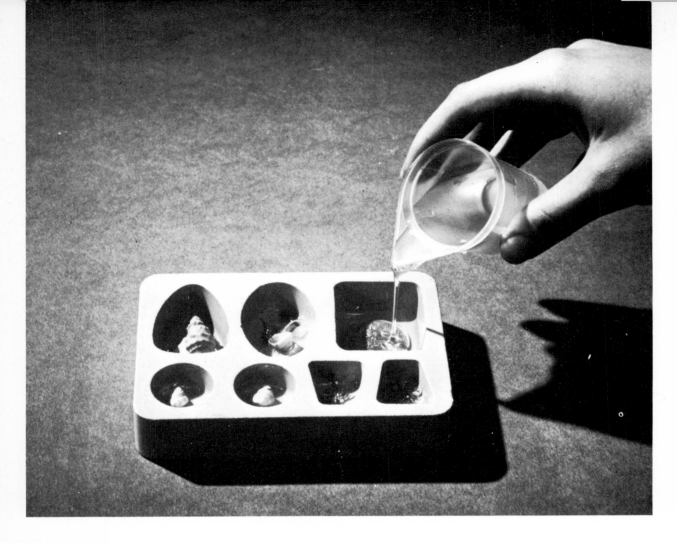

embedded as an integral part of the casting. Where facilities permit, metal jewelry mounts can be designed and made in conjunction with the resin ornaments. Manufactured fittings are obtainable in a wide range of styles for rings, brooches, bracelets and pendants to which resin shapes can be attached with clear adhesive (*figures 37 and 38*).

FIGURE 36 Pouring activated resin into ceramic moulds containing small objects for embedding
Turner Research Limited (Plasticraft)

FIGURE 37 Methods of securing
pendant shapes. *(a)* Jump-ring
passed through hole drilled in resin.
(b) Bell-cap attached with resin
adhesive. *(c)* Twisted wire encircling
pendant. *(d)* Jump-ring on shaped
wire embedded in resin. *(e)* Flexible
cord, leather thong or chain
embedded in resin

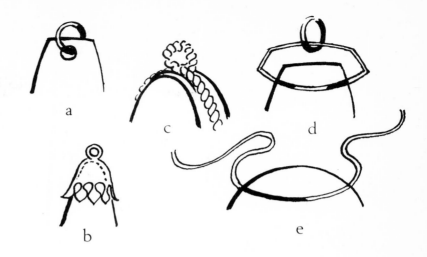

FIGURE 38 Ring and brooch
mounts. *Top row and below left*
Manufactured ring and brooch
fittings for mounting resin shapes.
Bottom row Ring shank cast into
resin. *(a)* Polythene strip shape.
(b) Ring shank in position for
pouring additional resin.
(c) Cast ring, polythene removed,
ready for further shaping if required

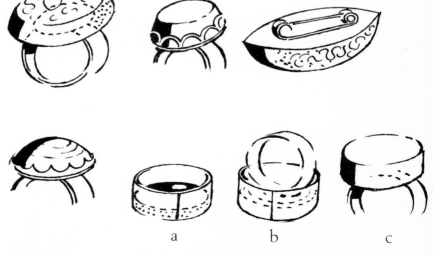

The following techniques for making resin jewelry are presented as basic exercises and further exploration along similar lines will reveal many creative possibilities. In the hands of an imaginative designer, coloured resin can be a bright decorative element; as contemporary as current trends in dress. In short, resin jewelry is of the twentieth century and has the gaiety and liveliness of the boutique.

FIGURE 39 Selection of resin jewelry with embedded objects and manufactured fittings *Turner Research Limited (Plasticraft)*

A *cabochon* is a term used in jewelry to describe a gemstone with a smooth, rounded dome as distinct from angular or faceted stones. The base is usually flat and can be oval, rectangular or even irregular in shape, while the dome may be shallow or steeply formed.

A resin cabochon suitable for ring or pendant can be shaped quite simply by means of a hand file, then smoothed and polished. Shallow blocks of coloured resin can be cast in thin layers, one above the other, to give the effect of laminations. This will produce concentric rings when shaped into a domed cabochon, and when cut across will show a striped or straight banded pattern. Blocks containing swirled or random colouring will present infinite colour variations when shaped and polished. Detailed procedure is described as follows.

Saw the resin blocks into smaller pieces, making cabochons of different sizes.

FIGURE 40   *(a)* Cast resin block. *(b)* Resin block sawn as required

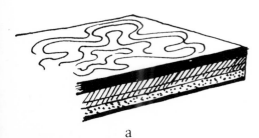

a

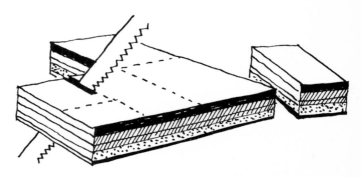

b

(a) Mark out shape on trimmed piece. Further sawing will quickly remove unwanted portions, to save filing.
(b) Clamp in a small table vice and file to desired shape, using forward cutting strokes.

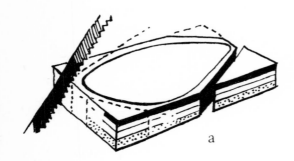

a

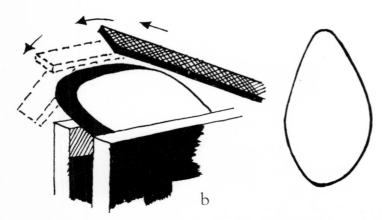

b

FIGURE 41

(a)　To aid further shaping, the resin shape can be fixed temporarily to a wooden stick with resin adhesive or a mixture of melted sealing wax and powdered shellac. Allow to set.

(b)　Stick can be held in a vice to file larger pieces *or*

(c)　Held in the hand to work smaller pieces.

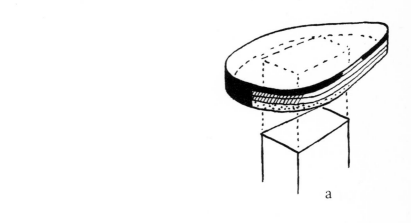

a

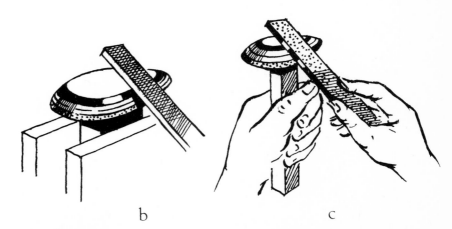

b

c

FIGURE 42

Top row Stages in shaping the dome profile of a pendant cabochon. Proceed in a series of step cuts. Finally, remove all remaining points.

Bottom row Plan and profile of: *(a)* symmetrical pear-drop cut. *(b)* An irregular, off-centre pendant.

PLATE 3 Examples of creative ► encapsulation

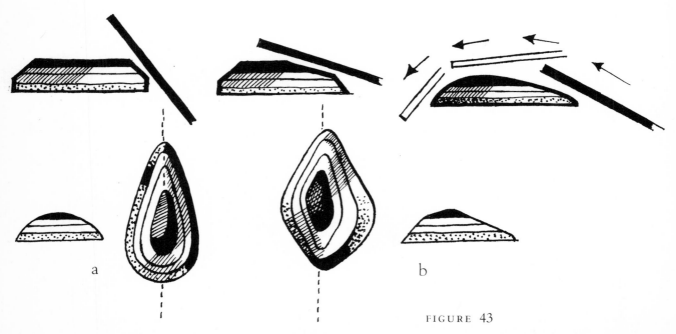

a

b

FIGURE 43

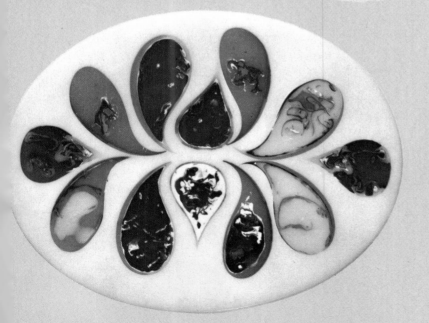

FIGURE 44

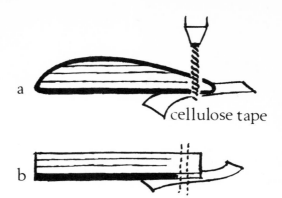

Drilling a hole for pendant loop and chain. A hand drill can be used. Cellulose adhesive tape fixed on the base will prevent resin chipping as the drill breaks through. *(a)* Hole can be drilled after shaping. *(b)* Hole drilled prior to shaping.

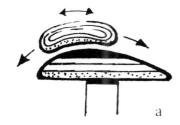

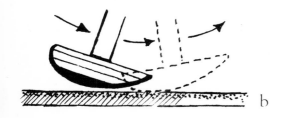

FIGURE 45

(a) Smoothing the cabochon dome with wet/dry abrasive papers wrapped round a pad of foam rubber for resilience.
(b) Polishing on a flat pad, rocking the cabochon in different directions. When completely polished, remove from stick and sand base until smooth. Polish if required.

The final stages of this method resemble cloissoné enamelling, where pools of colour are contained within areas formed by shallow retaining walls. In this case, shapes are formed in a wax mould by means of heated wires, producing raised patterns of resin which are cast at the same time as the supporting ground.

Materials for preparing moulds
Tobacco tins
Supply of wax (preferably dental wax)
Hot plate for melting wax in tin
Short lengths of wire, strong but bendable
A wooden handle e.g. pen-holder or piece of drilled dowel
Wire cutters
Small pair of round-nosed pliers
Gas ring or spirit lamp to heat hot plate and wire shapes

Procedure
Where a gas ring is not available a small spirit lamp will serve equally well and many types of hot plate can be constructed simply *(figure 46)*.

Heat the tobacco tin on the hot plate, gradually adding pieces of wax to make up to required level. The molten wax should occupy two-thirds of the depth of the tin, allowing space for layers of resin and glass fibre. When the wax is liquid remove from heat and paint a thin coating of wax up to the interior rim to prevent resin sticking to the tin. Allow to cool and solidify.

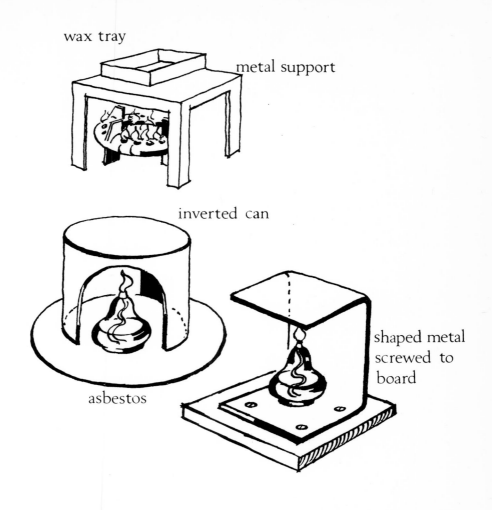

wax tray

metal support

inverted can

shaped metal screwed to board

asbestos

FIGURE 46   Appliances for heating wax and wire

With the round-nosed pliers, bend a series of self-contained shapes in the wire, allowing one end to project. Test the wire shapes on a flat surface to ensure they are level. Insert the projecting end of wire into a pen-holder or a hole drilled in the end of a wooden dowel. Wedge the wire firmly in place *(figure 47)*.

Heat the wire in a flame until warm but not too hot. Holding the handle steady, press the heated tool into the hardened tray of wax making an impression of the wire pattern *(figures 48a and b)*. If the impression is not of sufficient depth at the first application, re-heat the wire and place carefully into the same depression. Depending on requirements, the same pattern can be repeated or a variety of designs can be made in the same tray of wax.

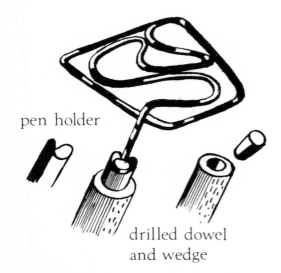

pen holder

drilled dowel
and wedge

FIGURE 47 Wire shape fixed into holder

FIGURE 48 *(a)* Wire heated in the flame of a spirit lamp.
(b) Heated wire pressed into wax

a

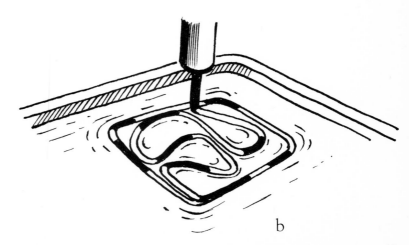

b

Making the resin casting

Mix a strongly coloured resin to form a positive boundary in the raised portions of the casting. Pour a covering layer over the wax, making sure that all indentations are uniformly filled. Cut a piece of glass fibre matting to fit in the tin and place it on the resin.

NOTE   Be sure to wear gloves when handling glass fibre. With a stiff brush, puddle the resin through the fibres to ensure even bonding. Allow to set. Repeat the glass fibre and resin treatment to provide further reinforcing layers (*figure 49*). Without the glass fibre the resin sheet would be brittle and liable to snap.

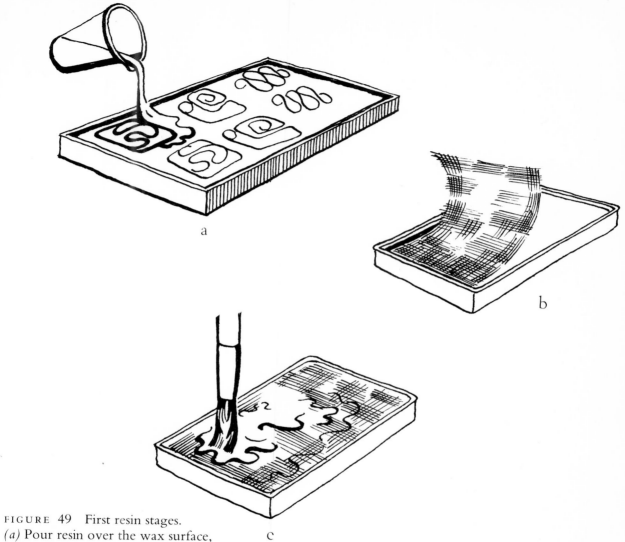

FIGURE 49 First resin stages.
(a) Pour resin over the wax surface,
filling pattern indentations.
(b) Glass fibre matting cut to size.
(c) Puddling the resin through the
matting

Further development

Carefully ease the hardened casting from the tin, if possible leaving the wax impressions for further use. Using a fine hacksaw blade, isolate the individual relief patterns conforming to the original wire shapes. Smooth edges with a file *(figure 50)*.

The final stages will allow many decorative possibilities, using coloured resin in opaque or translucent form. Apply the liquid resin in small droplets, either with a fine brush or a piece of stick, carefully filling the cavities until level, *(figure 51)*. It is advisable to proceed slowly and have several pieces on the go at the same time. Allow the colour in each small enclosure to set before filling an adjacent shape to prevent colours from running together. If desired, the completed piece may be sanded and polished. Finished examples can be used to make brooches or drilled for use as pendants.

FIGURE 50 *(a)* The reinforced resin sheet containing *cloissoné* patterns is lifted clear of the wax. *(b)* Cutting the designs from the sheet with a hacksaw. *(c)* Resin replica of wire shapes, ready for final processing

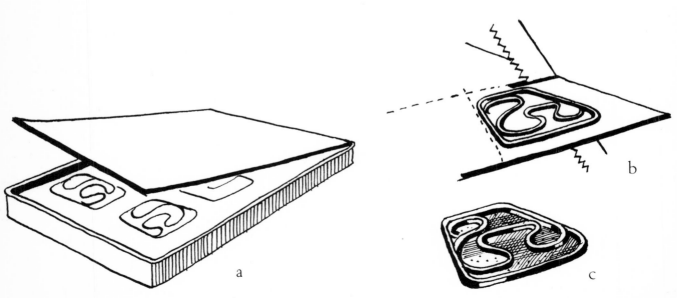

a

b

c

FIGURE 51 Drops of coloured
resin applied gradually with a brush
or stick

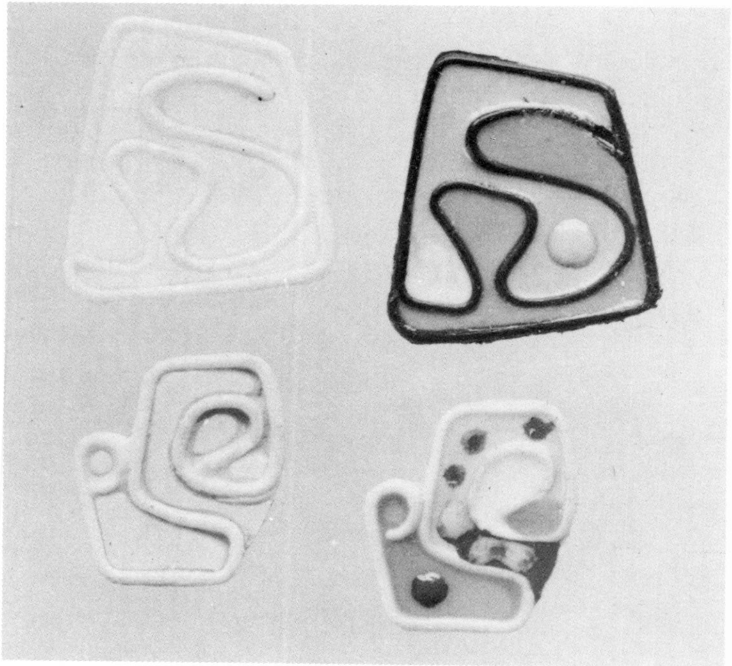

FIGURE 52 Examples of decorative
units made by the hot wire and wax
process. *Left* Basic resin casts.
Right Coloured resins added to
enclosed areas. Note the globules of
resin applied when the ground
surface had set

As an elaboration on the techniques using polythene bottle strips, described in the previous chapter, a more creative approach to resin jewelry is possible with this process. The simplicity of this method makes it an attractive proposition for either the junior craft room or for the mature designer in the home. Jewelry produced in this way often resembles enamelled or ceramic forms when polished.

Materials required
Flexible polythene bottles
Sharp craft knife
Roll of cellulose adhesive tape
Coloured resins

Procedure
Cut off tops of polythene bottles (do not throw these away, they make useful funnels for pouring resins). Cut away the base of the bottles leaving cylinder form. The bases can also be utilised as shallow mixing cups.

Cut open the cylinder from top to base and open out polythene to make a flat sheet. This can be fixed with thumbtacks at the edges to prevent curling when cutting into strips. Using a metal straight-edge, as a guide, cut a series of parallel strips 3mm to 6mm ($\frac{1}{8}$in. to $\frac{1}{4}$in.) wide, depending on the desired thickness of the resin.

Manipulate the strips into rhythmical patterns dictated by the flexibility of the material. Secure loose ends and detached loops to form a self-contained unit *(figure 53a and b)*. Seal the base with adhesive tape to prevent any leakage of resin. A few alternative patterns can be prepared at the same time.

two ends secured

free loop secured

FIGURE 53 A continuous polythene strip bent to shape and held in position with cellulose tape

Reference to the diagram will make clear the method used *(figure 54).*

(a) Fill in the areas between polythene walls with resin and allow to set.

(b) Remove polythene strips to isolate individual shapes. Arrange cast shapes in same order as before on a base of adhesive tape, leaving small gaps to correspond to thickness of polythene.

(c) Erect a further polythene strip around the shapes but slightly higher than before and seal junctions to make leak-proof.

a

b

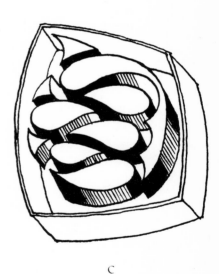

c

FIGURE 54

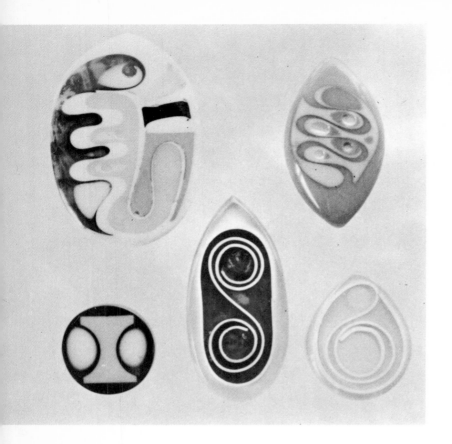

FIGURE 55 *Top left and right*
Completed pendant designs.
Below left Motif in coloured resin,
suitable for a ring.
Centre and below right Polythene
bottle strips embedded as decorative
whorls and loops, covered with
clear resin

Pour in a contrasting background of coloured resin
to flow between the shapes, forming an integrated resin
unit. The height of the liquid should be level with the
original shapes. When thoroughly set, remove polythene
walls and adhesive tape. Polish the resin castings and make
into jewelry by attaching to manufactured fittings with
epoxy resin adhesive or drill holes so that they can be
threaded on chains or leather thongs.

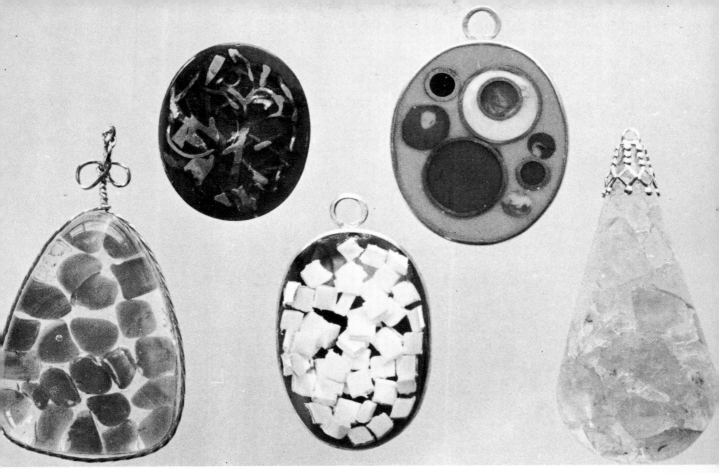

FIGURE 56 *Top left* Scraps of silver in resin, sanded and polished. *Top right* Silver tube sections and coloured resin, cast in silver bezel. *Bottom row* Tumble polished carnelians set in clear resin, setting from twisted gold wire. White plastic scraps on black resin ground, covered with clear resin, domed and polished. Fragments of translucent coloured resin embedded in clear resin, shaped and polished with bell-cap attached

77

Casting small sculptures

Three dimensional models and constructions can only be mentioned briefly within the scope of this book but the creative applications of resin in this field are wide. Many contemporary sculptors and designers are exploiting the inherent properties of plastics as an expressive medium and the use of polyester resins is assuming an important role as an art form. As the projects throughout this book are confined to those which can be produced in a home workshop or in a corner of a craft room, the techniques for reproducing only small reliefs and sculptures are introduced here to meet these limitations. More ambitious projects can be attempted where facilities permit.

Shallow relief models, such as the example illustrated *(figure 57)*, can be modelled initially in clay or *Plasticine* and a mould of plaster of paris of fine quality prepared for casting *(figure 58)*. Absorbent mould surfaces, such as plaster of paris, must be thoroughly sealed to prevent the liquid resin from seeping away into the mould material. Thin coatings of shellac, allowed to harden thoroughly between coats, followed by an application of wax, will prevent resin penetration and provide easy release from the mould. Prepare the resins in the usual way for casting and pour into the mould carefully to avoid formation of bubbles.

FIGURE 57 Resin casting from a
plaster mould. Relief head mounted
as a plaque on a coloured acrylic
sheet

FIGURE 58 Plaster of paris mould,
cast from a shallow relief model in
Plasticine

For multiple reproduction of small models such as chess pieces, or casting sculptural forms, hot-melt flexible vinyl moulds are suitable for resin casting. Vinyl-based compounds are produced to melt at different temperatures ranging from approximately 120°C (248°F) to 170°C (338°F) and can be obtained in grades of flexibility; soft, medium, and hard. Medium or hard mould compound in the higher temperature range of melting should be used for casting polyester resins in order to withstand the heat rise in curing. Blocks of vinyl hot-melt or remelt-able rubber compounds, manufactured under various trade names, are available from suppliers of resins and craft materials. These hot-melt compounds can be melted down and re-used several times but have a limited life due to eventual decomposition. A range of ready-made moulds are also obtainable for anyone lacking facilities for mould preparation but these must be of the type specifically for resin casting as many of the rubber moulds intended for casting plaster models would be unsuitable.

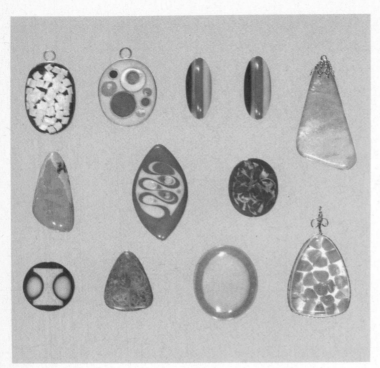

MOULD MAKING PROCEDURE

The hot-melt compound retains a high temperature during pouring so it is important to ensure that the original model material will not melt at the same temperature as the molten solution. Heat sensitive or brittle materials should be warmed slowly, prior to pouring the mould compound, to counteract any variation in temperature. Metallic forms should also be heated to prevent premature cooling of the mould compound when it contacts the metal. Porous forms should be sealed as already described but it is not necessary to coat with releasing wax. One-piece moulds are suitable for reproducing small objects or carvings providing the forms are simplified and possess minimum detail or undercutting. More complicated models would require a mould prepared in two halves.

◀ PLATE 4 *Above* Resin shapes suitable for jewelry. *Below* Beadwork motif, worked by Clare Myers, embedded in resin.

To melt the compound, a double heating container is normally used. This is constructed on the glue-pot or double saucepan principle. Heating is done without water in the outer pan, thus forming hot air circulation around the vessel in which melting takes place *(figure 59)*. It is important that the containers used are capable of withstanding sustained application of heat.

To prepare the melt, cut the compound into small pieces and add to the container in easy stages, stirring occasionally to separate the lumps as melting occurs. This should be a gradual process to prevent burning the compound, and melting time may be from half to three-quarters of an hour for one pound weight of compound. Cover with a loose-fitting lid to contain fumes and retain full effectiveness of the mixture. When the required volume has reached an even, molten state, remove the pan from heat source and allow to stand until the contents have settled into a smooth consistency. The pouring temperature should be less than melting point to prevent bubbling but the mixture must not be allowed to gel.

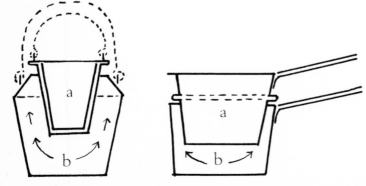

FIGURE 59 Two types of melting vessels for rubber compounds.
(a) Inner melting container.
(b) Hot air circulation

Construct a retaining wall around the original model, sealing any joints with gummed paper strip to prevent leakage, or stand the model in a can of suitable proportions *(figures 60a and b)*. Slowly pour the molten rubber compound into the space between model and retaining wall, allowing the level to rise until the model is submerged about 13mm ($\frac{1}{2}$in.) *(figure 60c)*. Leave until the compound is completely cold, which may take several hours depending on the thickness, before removing the mould from the container. Carefully extract the original model, leaving a hollow, negative replica.

FIGURE 60 *(a)* Original model suitably contained. *(b)* Joints sealed with tape and modelling clay. *(c)* Do not pour rubber directly onto the model

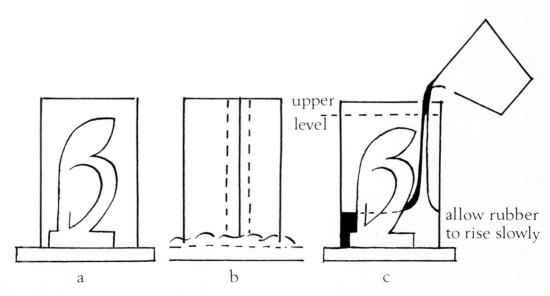

upper
level

allow rubber
to rise slowly

a   b   c

Use of a cold curing process provides an alternative method of preparing rubber moulds for resin casting and has a wider range of applications. One of the main advantages of this method is that melting and heating appliances are dispensed with as the silicone rubber is supplied in liquid form to which a catalyst is added in correct proportions. During mixing complete dispersion of the catalyst is essential and for this reason it is coloured to show uniform blending within the base liquid. Stirring should be done thoroughly with a palette knife, spatula or rotary whisk.

Viscosity of the mixture can be adjusted by adding recommended thinners to the uncatalysed base liquid without affecting the curing properties of the material. The variable viscosity is a further advantage in this process and it can be poured over the three-dimensional model or sculpture to be reproduced, as outlined in the previous method. It can also be obtained as a thick paste which is applied with a brush or small trowel. The paste consistency is ideally suited for producing a rubber mould impression of vertical textured surfaces such as rock formations, fossil imprints, relief sculptures and incised lettering. Used in this way the possibilities of this mould material are extensive as it can be brushed into the most complex forms and undercut surfaces without sagging or distortion. When fully cured the flexible rubber mould can be easily peeled away from the model or sculptured surface. The mould can be used repeatedly for casting resin reproductions but, unlike the vinyl hot melt compounds, the silicone rubber cannot be reconstituted for further use.

Thin moulds must be adequately supported prior to casting to prevent internal bulging or distortion of the cavity shape. One method of providing support is to surround the mould with several layers of damp tissue-paper and then add a coating of plaster of paris (*figure 61*). The paper tissue will allow movement when manipulating the resin cast from a one-piece mould. Thicker, or less flexible rubber moulds may be self-supporting.

FIGURE 61 A method of supporting the rubber mould in a rigid position for pouring resin. The outer layer is plaster of paris; the inner one is damp paper which cushions the mould

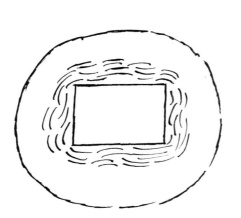

mould opening

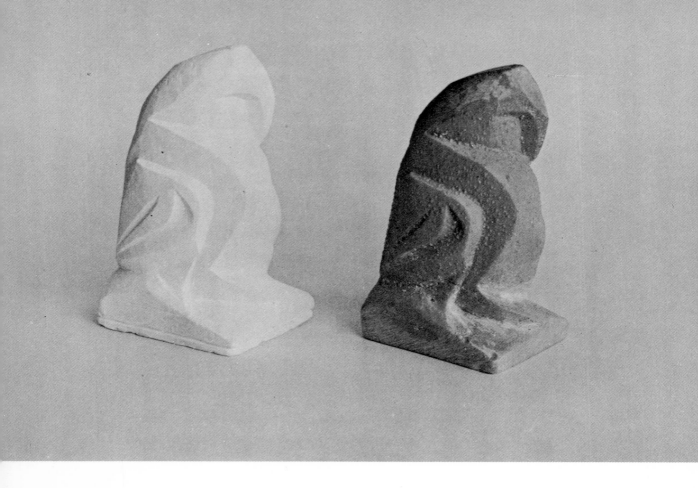

FIGURE 62 Decorative bird form.
Left The original model carved
from plaster of paris.
Right Reproduction in resin, cast
from a rubber mould. Note the
exact repetition of the silhouette
forms

Prepare a quantity of resin but cut down the amount of hardener to resin in the mixture to avoid high exotherm during curing. This will lessen the risk of cracking in the resin cast and prevent any partial melting of the mould by excessive heat. If this occurs, parts of the mould may stick and break away when the casting is removed and this would render the mould unfit for further use.

Opaque or translucent colours can be added to the resin mixture or metallic fillers introduced. A range of metal simulants are possible in this way, such as aluminium, brass, bronze and copper. Other powdered fillers such as chalk, slate and crushed quartz sand will also provide variations in colour and texture in the finished castings.

Slowly pour the resin mixture into the mould and tap repeatedly to remove air bubbles. Shake the mould to force resin into any cavities or depressions. When the mould is filled, remove it to a well-ventilated storage place where it can remain undisturbed until the resin has thoroughly hardened. Since the mould is flexible, there should be no difficulty in removing the finished casting. The same mould can be used again and again, producing identical castings.

FIGURE 63 Aluminium lathe turnings embedded in tinted resin. Intended as a sculptural form, to be mounted on a plinth or supported on a metal rod. Changing light and viewpoint present a varied play of light and shade on the metal forms

Additional projects

Tiles and small decorative panels can be produced by casting raised containing walls for subsequent pools of colour. A V-shaped indentation is cut in a tray of wax with a sharp knife, tracing the outline of a suitable pattern. Prepare the wax beforehand in shallow tins as described in the chapter on resin jewelry. A resin casting from the wax, reinforced with glass fibre, will provide a relief network for application of coloured resin *(figure 64)*. By careful extraction of the casting from the wax tray, to avoid breaking the wax, the panel or tile can be reproduced for arrangement as a repeating motif.

FIGURE 64 *Left* Linear pattern
carved in a tray of wax. *Right* Resin
casting from the wax mould. The
original wax indentations are now
raised enclosures to contain coloured
resins

89

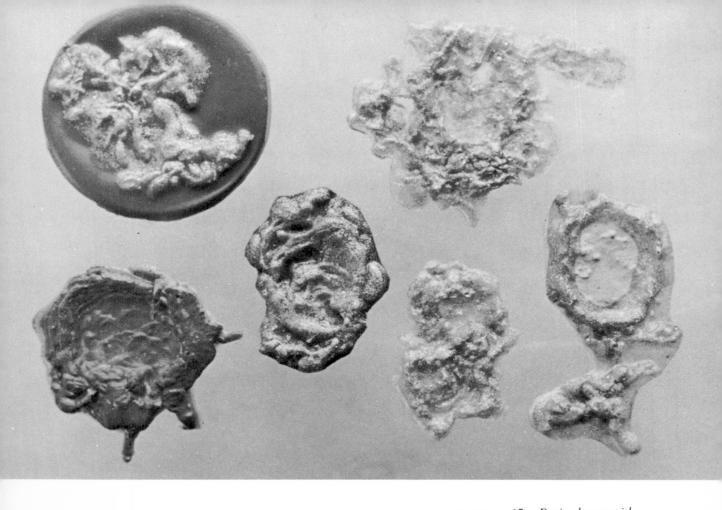

FIGURE 65 *Resin shapes with*
metallic powder fillers cast from wax
impressions (see *figure 66*). Impressions
can be made in soft wax with articles
such as cinders, tree bark and metal
scraps. Cast shapes can be developed
as sculptures or used for jewelry. For
example: the cast shape further
embedded on a resin background
(top left)

For an alternative method of making a decorative panel, cut open a polythene bottle and tack it flat on a board, or use a sheet of waxed glass. Enclose a rectangular or circular shape with modelling clay, pressing it down firmly to prevent leakage. Pour a thin film of resin as a base and build up several glass fibre reinforcing layers. Using materials such as string or plastic covered wire of sufficient thickness to form a shallow relief, press them on the resin base before it reaches a gel state. In this way the string or wire can be manipulated into patterns by sliding on the base, ensuring uniform adhesion and leak free enclosures. Curves and spirals can easily be formed with these materials. When the base has set hard, fill in the spaces with coloured resins. Simulated stained-glass panels can be produced in this way, using translucent pools of coloured resin.

Mosaic pieces in opaque or translucent colours can be cut from sheets of cast resin. Wax the surface of a piece of glass and build a shallow retaining wall around it. Pour in coloured resin to the required thickness of the mosaic pieces and cover with a further sheet of waxed glass or polythene sheet. Covering the resin in this way will prevent shrinkage and save the need for polishing. Before the resin has set too hard, cut the mosaic pieces with a sharp knife by scoring to the base. Leave until completely hard. When required the mosaic pieces can be separated and arranged in attractive patterns.

FIGURE 66   Small tray of wax showing impression of textured form, prepared for resin casting

Resin makes an excellent adhesive and binding agent for all forms of mosaic and inlay work. Used in conjunction with thin slabs of polished stones, attractive trays and table surfaces can be produced. Collage materials such as fabrics, dried grasses, wood and pebbles can also be successfully incorporated with coloured resins.

Many other creative uses of polyester resin are possible and it is hoped that the technique and examples shown will stimulate further ideas.

FIGURE 68   Decorative relief
panel.   *Left* Intaglio shapes carved
in plaster of paris with a wooden
frame as an additional containing
wall.   *Right* Panel cast from the
mould in two stages. First the
coloured resin was poured into
the mould cavities and allowed to
set. Then a contrasting resin
background was added and reinforced

Further reading

Plastics for Schools P. J. CLARK Allman and Son, London
Plastics as an Art Form THELMA R. NEWMAN Pitman and
Sons Ltd, London

PUBLICATIONS AND TECHNICAL INFORMATION LEAFLETS

ICI Plastics Division, Bessemar Road, Welwyn Garden City, Herts
Information on uses of plastics for schools

Turner Research Ltd, Plastics Division, Jubilee Terrace, Leeds LS6 2XH
*Instruction leaflets on embedding, preservation, moulds and
cold-setting enamels*

Trylon Ltd, Woolaston, Northants
*Instruction leaflets on embedding, uses of glass fibre. Polyester
handbook*

Alec Tiranti Ltd, 72 Charlotte Street, London WIP 2AJ
Technical booklet, 'Flexible mould making with Vinamould'

Vinatex Ltd, Special Products Division, Nelson House,
19 West Street, Carshalton, Surrey
Data on hot melt compounds

Griffin Biological Laboratories Ltd, 113 Lavender Hill, Tonbridge, Kent
*Information leaflets on Kristablick process. Embedding
techniques and colour preservation in flowers*

Strand Glass Co Ltd, Brentway Trading Estate, Brentford, Middlesex
Information on resins and glass fibre

Suppliers

Embedding kits with resin, moulds and colour pigments
Fred Aldous Ltd, The Handicrafts Centre, 37 Lever Street, Manchester
E. J. Arnold, (School Suppliers) Butterley Street, Leeds
Bondaglass Limited, 158–164 Ravenscroft Road, Beckenham, Kent (also **glass fibre**)

Silicone rubber for mould making
Dow Corning Limited, Educational Suppliers, Hopkin and Williams, Ducie Street, Manchester 1

Resins, colour pigments, glass fibre. Preservation and embedding kits for botanical and biological specimens
Griffin and George Ltd, Technical Studies Group, Ealing Road, Alperton, Wembley, Middlesex

Resins and embedding kits, glass fibre, silicone rubber mould materials
Isopon Interchemicals, Industrial Estate, Maylands Avenue, Hemel Hempstead, Herts

Resins, glass fibre, colour pigments
Strand Glass Co Ltd, Brentway Trading Estate, Brentford, Middlesex

Resins, glass fibre, mould compounds
Alec Tiranti Ltd, 72 Charlotte Street, London W1P 2AJ

Resins, glass fibre, fillers, colour pigments
Trylon Ltd, Wollaston, Northants

Plasticraft embedding kit, resins, colour pigments, remeltable rubber, cold-setting enamels
Turner Research Ltd, Plastics Division, Jubilee Terrace, Leeds

Additional sources of supply
Complete resin craft kits, manufactured under various
trade names, are obtainable from lapidary dealers,
craft and hobby shops, and some department stores

USA

The following suppliers carry a complete line of plastics
supplies and will fill mail orders:

Resin Coatings Corporation
14940 NW 25 Court, Opa Locka, Florida 33054

Polyproducts Corporation
Order Department, Room 25
13810 Nelson Avenue, Detroit, Michigan 48227

CANADA

Waldor Enterprises Limited (Division of *Ren Plastics Inc*)
2580 Wharton Glen Avenue
Mississauga, Ontario, Canada